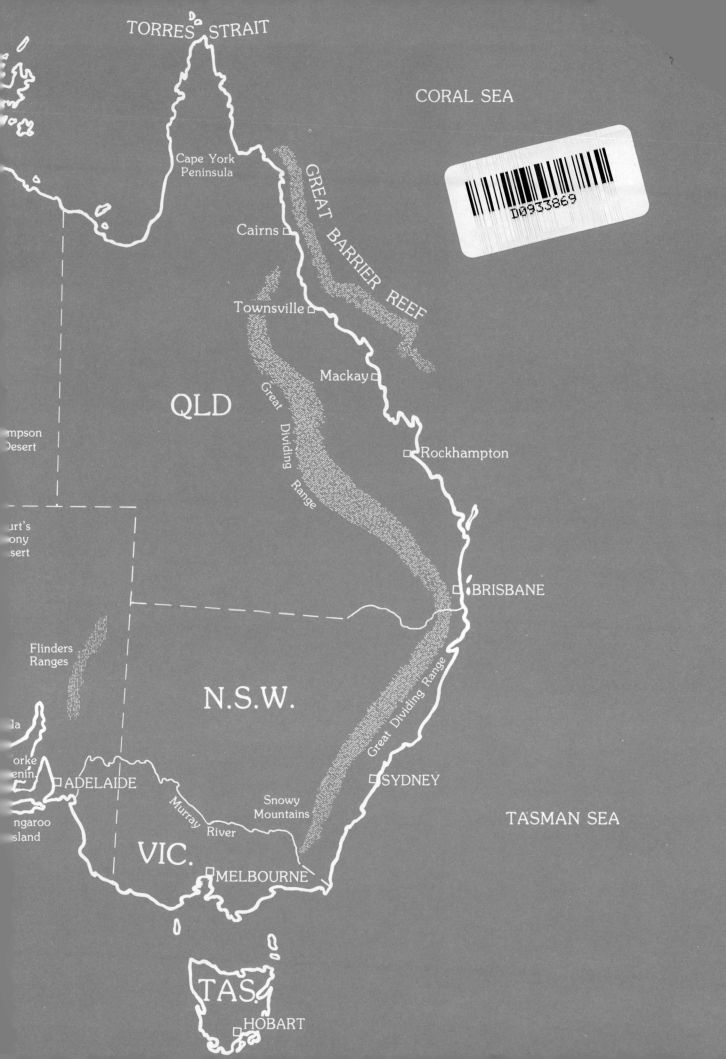

TORRES STRAIT

CORAL SEA

Cape York
Peninsula

GREAT BARRIER REEF

Cairns □

QLD

Townsville □

Great
Dividing
Range

Mackay □

Rockhampton □

□ BRISBANE

mpson
Desert

urt's
ony
sert

Flinders
Ranges

N.S.W.

Great Dividing Range

la

orke
enin.

□ ADELAIDE

SYDNEY

ngaroo
sland

Murray River

Snowy
Mountains

TASMAN SEA

VIC.

□ MELBOURNE

TAS.

HOBART □

SCENIC AUSTRALIA

SCENIC AUSTRALIA

Jocelyn Burt

RIGBY

ORD RIVER, WESTERN AUSTRALIA

Contents

National Library of Australia
Cataloguing-in-Publication entry

Burt, Jocelyn.
  Scenic Australia.

  ISBN 0 7270 0646 0.

  1. Australia—Description and travel. I. Title.

919.4'04

RIGBY LIMITED • ADELAIDE • SYDNEY
MELBOURNE • BRISBANE • PERTH
First published in 1978
Copyright © 1978 by Jocelyn Burt
All rights reserved
Wholly designed and set up in Australia
Printed in Hong Kong

YAMBA, NEW SOUTH WALES

Seashores and Islands

Australia is bound by 38 000 kilometres of scenically diverse shoreline washed by seven seas: the Indian, Southern, and Pacific oceans, and the Timor, Arafura, Coral, and Tasman seas. Much of the coast in the more populated east and south-east is accessible either by road or track, but in other parts of the continent, especially in the north-west, it is still largely virgin ground, well protected on one side by dangerous reefs and tides and on the other by difficult, often treacherous terrain.

Some of Australia's grandest scenery lies in her rugged coastline with its spectacular cliffs and rock formations. Fortunately, many of the most beautiful areas can be viewed quite easily from special lookouts set aside along the road. Along the Eyre Highway in South Australia, for example, there are magnificent views of the ninety metres high perpendicular cliffs that edge the Great Australian Bight. At Port Campbell in Victoria there are more splendid cliffs from which one may watch the restless sea ceaselessly pounding the bizarre landforms of stacks and arches that lie offshore.

Australia's magnificent wide beaches are the most popular of all her coastal features. With their fine sand and rolling surf, they have long been famous throughout the world for their beauty. They sweep right around the coast, giving way in places to rocky headlands and cliffs, or to mud flats laced with networks of mangroves. Some run virtually unbroken for long distances of well over 100 kilometres; others are pocket-sized and secluded, tucked away between areas of rock.

Quiet inlets and coastal lagoons provide an effective contrast to the dramatic sweep of beach or cliff-face. Places like Mallacoota Inlet, the Coorong, and Merimbula offer much enchantment in their tranquillity.

The colours of the sea vary enormously, depending on climate and location. The deep greens and blues of the southern coastal waters change to vibrant turquoise and aquamarine in the warmer north. In some places, particularly around the south-west coast of Western Australia, the colours often appear in contrasting bands or stripes, varying from the palest of greens near the shore to a dark inky blue further out. The sea's brilliant and changeable colours are further accentuated by the warmer hues of cliffs, rocks, and sand, from the yellow sandstone cliffs of South Australia's Fleurieu Peninsula to the rusty browns and brilliant reds of the rocky escarpments in north-western Australia. The sands of the beaches and dunes all around the coast range in colour from golden or white to an occasional rich terracotta.

Australia's shores are fringed by hundreds of islands of all sizes—from small outcrops of rocks, shallow mud flats, or low-lying coral islets to vast mountainous masses. Most of the islands, whether single or grouped, are continental in origin: they were once part of the mainland, but became separated from it millions of years ago by submergence, faulting, and erosion. Some of the most beautiful lie off the north-eastern coast of Queensland. With their forested slopes and lovely beaches lapped by calm, clear seas, it is hardly surprising that many of them have became popular holiday playgrounds for thousands of Australians and overseas visitors. But there is more to this sub-tropical paradise than its beautiful islands. Extending for 2000 kilometres, from the Torres Strait in the north to just south of Gladstone, is one of the great wonders of the world: the Great Barrier Reef. Here extraordinary coral reefs of breathtaking beauty give shelter to an enormous variety of marine life, providing Australia with a priceless natural heritage.

NEAR APOLLO BAY, VICTORIA

TERRIGAL, NEW SOUTH WALES
The many wide, sweeping beaches of the Sydney metropolitan area are justly famous. This lovely stretch of coast at Terrigal lies 100 kilometres north of the city.

Previous pages:
PORT CAMPBELL, VICTORIA
Fashioned by waves and weather over the centuries, these spectacular formations known as the Twelve Apostles are now part of the Port Campbell National Park that covers about 32 kilometres of coastline in western Victoria. There are many other fascinating landforms in this area.

KANGAROO ISLAND, SOUTH AUSTRALIA
Balancing on top of a domed granite headland in the far south-west of the island are the Remarkable Rocks, an extraordinary and dramatic collection of boulders riddled with indentations and yawning caverns. Kangaroo Island, Australia's third largest island, covers 1600 square kilometres and lies off the Fleurieu and Yorke peninsulas. There are four small towns, the largest being Kingscote, and access from the mainland is by air or vehicular ferry which leaves from Port Adelaide. Tourists come in large numbers each year to see the coastal scenery for which the island is renowned.

NEAR ALBANY, WESTERN AUSTRALIA

Situated about 20 kilometres south of Albany is the Torndirrup National Park, which covers part of the promontory bordering King George Sound. With its wild rocky slopes pushing boldly into the turbulent sea and dramatic coastal features like the Blowhole and the Natural Bridge, the scenery in this region is both unusual and arresting. Visitors should allow plenty of time to enjoy its many attractions. Fishing from the rocks can be very dangerous because of the unexpected king waves that from time to time sweep over the shore. Not far from this spot is the Albany Whaling Station.

CAIRNS, QUEENSLAND

This tranquil view from the town's lawn-edged Esplanade is enhanced by the soft light of early dawn. At low tide waterbirds can be seen feeding in the shallows. Nestling in the foothills of the Atherton Tableland on the coast of tropical north-east Queensland, 1863 kilometres from Brisbane, Cairns is situated in one of the most beautiful natural settings in Australia. With the district's superb scenery, the excellent fishing available, and the warm climate, it is not surprising that people come here in their thousands to escape the cold southern winters.

MERIMBULA, NEW SOUTH WALES

This lovely holiday resort scattered around a picturesque inlet lies 470 kilometres south of Sydney, in the area popularly called the 'Sapphire Coast' because of its brilliantly coloured seas. Through the trees that line the roads meandering along the cliff tops, tantalising glimpses of superb vistas can be seen. Commercial oyster farms flourish here, and as the tide goes out the neat lines of the oyster beds are clearly apparent. Merimbula was opened in 1855 as a port to serve the rural community and the gold diggers en route to Kiandra.

TESSELLATED PAVEMENT, TASMANIA

Some of Australia's most celebrated landforms lie on the Tasman Peninsula in south-east Tasmania. The Tasman Peninsula is linked by a thread of land at Eaglehawk Neck to the Forestier Peninsula; and one of its greatest attractions is the famous Tessellated Pavement, situated near the hotel at Eaglehawk Neck. This geological curiosity looks very much as if it has been artificially constructed. Long-ago earth movements fractured the fine sandstone rocks into their present shapes, then waves carrying sand and gravel gradually flattened them to give the characteristic 'pavement' effect. Some of the stone 'tiles' have neat shallow basins formed by a chemical action of the sea water.

Top left:

MARIA ISLAND, TASMANIA

Lying offshore from Orford and Triabunna on the east coast, this island was once the site of a harsh convict penitentiary. Many of the historic buildings dating from the convict days still stand, but today Maria Island is a national park with hiking paths leading to many lovely scenic spots.

Bottom left:

CAPE LEEUWIN, WESTERN AUSTRALIA

This windswept headland of craggy granite lies in the far south-west corner of the State.

Above:

ELLISTON, SOUTH AUSTRALIA

The attractive fishing town of Elliston is situated on the west coast of Eyre Peninsula, 724 kilometres from Adelaide. From the cliff-top lookout at the edge of the town one can see to the north and south grand panoramas of cliffs plunging to rocky shores and stretches of smooth, clean sand. All along this coast there are many spots that afford spectacular views. One of the best-known is Point Labatt, home for a large colony of sea lions, some 50 kilometres north of Elliston near Streaky Bay.

17

PRINCE OF WALES ISLAND, QUEENSLAND

Situated near Thursday Island in the Torres Strait, between Cape York and Papua-New Guinea, is Prince of Wales Island. At 180 square kilometres, it is the largest island in the area. Today only a handful of Melanesian islanders and Europeans live there, and Prince of Wales Island slumbers peacefully under the tropical sun, resting from the turbulent years of its past. During the last century it saw one of the strangest of Australia's many shipwreck incidents which later involved the rescue of a Scottish woman who for years had lived with the island's native inhabitants, the Kowraregas. The islanders once believed that anyone with a pale skin was a *lamar* — a spirit in human form who must immediately be returned to the land of spirits if the tribe were not to be stricken by disease. However, if the *lamar* showed a resemblance to a deceased relative, its life was spared. When 18-year-old Barbara Thompson, sole survivor of a shipping disaster, was discovered by Kowraregas intent on plundering the vessel, she was thought to be the spirit daughter of a chieftain. In 1849 she was rescued by Owen Stanley of H.M.S. *Rattlesnake*. On her return to civilisation she was able to give valuable information about the islanders' customs, which were quite different from those of the Australian Aborigines. Twenty-three years later the entire Kowrarega tribe was massacred.

GREAT KEPPEL ISLAND, QUEENSLAND

The sun sets over the sea at Fishermans Beach, Great Keppel Island. The biggest of a group of islands in Keppel Bay, Great Keppel is 40 kilometres from Rockhampton and only 14 kilometres from the nearest point on the mainland. With its 1450 hectares of attractive bushland, it is one of the larger islands of the Great Barrier Reef. Nearby is North Keppel Island, only slightly smaller in size. From Great Keppel's highest point of 153 metres, there are glorious views across the water to other islands and the rugged contours of the mountain range that hides Rockhampton. The island's outstanding feature is its beaches, which are probably the finest of all the settled islands along the Queensland coast.

Seen from the air, long white stretches of sand sweep from one rocky headland to another, some curving elegantly, others straight and wide enough to take a landing aircraft. Unlike many of the northern islands of Australia, where low tides reveal ugly mud patches, Great Keppel's retreating seas expose only sand. At Fishermans Beach there is a resort that offers many facilities to holiday-makers. There is also an airstrip on the island.

19

High Country

Australia is not only the world's smallest continent, but also its flattest, with an average elevation of only about 300 metres. As the land mass was formed so early in the geological history of the world, the elements have had plenty of time to smooth and wear down the last of the great mountainous upheavals without further interruption. Today, many of Australia's elevations known as 'mountains' are really no more than hills when compared with other mountains in the world. Seen from the air, most of the ranges appear as a series of gentle folds, rather crumpled and creased in aspect.

The backbone of Australia, and its only continental mountain chain, is the Great Dividing Range. This consists of a series of ranges, plateaux, and spurs that stretch from Cape York in the far north to Victoria and Tasmania in the south. Like a defiant barrier, the Great Divide separates the fertile east coast from the vast tract of dry inland plains. Some of its peaks easily reach to 1600 metres: Queensland's highest, at 1611 metres, is the rainforested Mount Bartle Frere, while Victoria's Mount Bogong, with its eucalypt-covered slopes, rises to 1983 metres. But the highest country of the Great Divide—and of all Australia—lies in the Snowy Mountains of New South Wales, where the craggy, boulder-studded Mount Kosciusko lords it over the ranges at 2330 metres.

The so-called Australian Alps, of which the Snowy Mountains form a part, are not alpine in the true sense of the word. Geologically speaking, they are not young enough. But although they are old and well-worn, their terrain is far from gentle. There are many places, often inconspicuous at a distance, where steep ravines act as formidable barriers, and vertical walls of craggy granite plunge suddenly to dizzying depths. In winter the higher regions of the Alps, both in Victoria and New South Wales, are well covered with snow.

Of all Australia's mountains, those in south-west Tasmania most resemble classic alpine scenery. With their serrated ridges and peaks rearing above glacial lakes and rugged plateaux, these ranges form part of an extensive and very beautiful wilderness area.

Other high country in Australia differs totally from that of the Great Dividing Range. Numerous hills sprawl over the north-west and central region. Rising abruptly from the plains, their old, dry-looking slopes are covered in rubble that supports little plant life. Often they are topped with great collars of rock. In the brilliantly coloured but formidable Kimberleys of north-western Australia, a few of the ranges reach a height of around 1000 metres. This region lies in the tropical belt that has only two seasons, the Wet and the Dry; and the ranges adopt quite a different character in each. During the rainless months between May and December, the land becomes increasingly dry and dusty and most of the vegetation, baked under the hot sun, turns to yellow and brown. But with the coming of the monsoonal rains the region pulsates with new life and freshness, and green colours dominate everywhere.

The most impressive high country in south-western Australia is the Stirling Range, which, although it has no great height, looks quite spectacular with its steep slopes rising suddenly from the surrounding flat plain. South Australia's most important mountain system is that comprising the Mount Lofty and Flinders ranges. The Mount Lofty Range starts as the picturesque, gently-rolling Adelaide Hills and eventually gives way to the rugged and magnificent Flinders. The latter ultimately fall away to the arid country of the northern plains, near Lake Frome.

FROM THE TOP OF CRADLE MOUNTAIN, TASMANIA

Top left:
SNOWY MOUNTAINS, NEW SOUTH WALES
One of the best places to see the Kosciusko Range is from the Alpine Way as it crosses the Swampy Plains.

Bottom left:
THREDBO, NEW SOUTH WALES
Tucked away in the Snowy Mountains, 207 kilometres from Canberra, Thredbo village is part of the Kosciusko National Park, which incorporates the highest mountain country in Australia. The skifields here offer many challenging runs for advanced skiers during the winter months.

Above:
MOUNT McKAY, VICTORIA
Mount McKay rises over the high plains, beyond the ski resort of Falls Creek. In winter this high country becomes a wonderful white world full of exquisite beauty waiting to be explored by the cross-country skier. Mounds of ice fashioned into fantastic shapes glitter in the sun, and gum trees bend under their burdens of snow, while the windward side of every protruding branch and twig is laced by blizzard-driven ice. When the wind stirs in the trees, the silence of the plain is broken by the sound of frozen gum leaves tinkling like charms on a bracelet.

23

TWEED VALLEY, NEW SOUTH WALES
The jagged peak of Mount Warning dominates the Tweed Valley in the far north of the State.

Previous pages:
BRIGHT, VICTORIA
Every autumn the town of Bright, 305 kilometres north-east of Melbourne, holds a festival to celebrate the beauty of the season; and at this time thousands of visitors come to see the glorious display of colourful trees. This is Centenary Park, one of Bright's many beauty spots.

MOUNT MACEDON, VICTORIA
Rising to 1013 metres, this once volcanic mountain lies 64 kilometres north-west of Melbourne. At its peak stands a giant cross, erected privately as a memorial to those who lost their lives during the first World War. Many years ago the area developed as a fashionable summer resort for Melburnians who wished to escape the stifling heat of the city. It even boasted a summer residence for the State Governor. Today Mount Macedon is still a popular resort, well-known for its beautiful homes and gardens—and for the magnificent colours of its trees in autumn.

FALLS CREEK, VICTORIA

Situated 378 kilometres from Melbourne and only three-quarters of an hour's drive from the alpine town of Mount Beauty in the Kiewa Valley, this popular winter resort has much to offer skiers. The slopes rise to 1800 metres and there is a wide assortment of ski-tows. Australia was one of the first countries in the world to make skiing a sport. It was introduced by some Scandinavian miners in the 1860s to help pass the time in the snowbound gold town of Kiandra, and since then it has been 'discovered' by many Australians.

STIRLING RANGE, WESTERN AUSTRALIA

Rising abruptly over plains studded with blackboys and low-growing eucalypts, the Stirling Range is seen here bathed in soft afternoon sunlight. This range, situated about 90 kilometres north of Albany in the south-west of the State, is an important national park. The region is particularly rich in wildflowers which adorn the ground in bright profusion throughout the spring months. There are some challenging hiking tracks that wind their way up to the rugged, stony-faced ridges and peaks. The highest peak, Bluff Knoll, rises to 1109 metres, and in winter sometimes wears a small mantle of snow.

KIMBERLEY COUNTRY, WESTERN AUSTRALIA
Like great battlements, the cliffs of the Carr Boyd Ranges, near the Lake Argyle tourist village, rear over the valleys to form part of the floodwater catchment of the Ord River. The colours of the ranges change constantly as the sun moves across the sky: from rich rust hues and rose pinks to soft purples and earthy browns. In the hotter months of the Dry season the colours are often softened by heat haze. Much of this area is inaccessible to man.

OVENS VALLEY, VICTORIA
Guarded by beautiful mountains, this fertile area nestles in the Alps of north-eastern Victoria. Through the valley flows the Ovens River, its clear, sparkling waters fed by the melting snows of the high plains around Mount Hotham and Mount Feathertop. Each season is marked with vivid clarity. In spring the sweet-smelling wattles herald warm days ahead, and in summer lush green growth covers the valleys and foothills. Then come spectacular autumn days, when the valley glows with the brilliantly-coloured leaves of the deciduous trees; and finally, in winter, dazzling white caps of snow cover the surrounding mountain peaks.

TCHUPPALLA FALLS, QUEENSLAND

Lying deep in rainforest, yet only a short walk from the road, the Tchuppalla Falls consist of a series of waterfalls that cascade down a steep rocky slope in the Palmerston National Park. A sign-posted walking path leads to both the Tchuppalla and the Wallacha falls, winding through luxuriant vegetation where sunlight filters softly through the canopy of leaves. The Palmerston National Park flanks the Palmerston Highway, where it protects a narrow strip of tropical rainforest. The entire route from Innisfail to Millaa Millaa on the Atherton Tableland is one of the loveliest drives in Queensland.

ATHERTON TABLELAND, QUEENSLAND

The Atherton Tableland, situated at the base of Cape York Peninsula, averages a height of approximately 760 metres above sea-level. Much of the tableland has been cleared of its tropical rainforest to make room for primary industry, and there are now many scenes like this one, near Malanda, where undulating pasture is broken only by small groups of remaining trees. The task of clearing the land has been an exacting one, and it is a task which still continues—much to the alarm of conservationists, as there are very few large tracts of rainforest left in Queensland.

MORIALTA GORGE, SOUTH AUSTRALIA

Throughout the Mount Lofty Ranges there are numerous reserves and national parks, some of them very close to the city of Adelaide. Lying immediately behind the suburb of Rostrevor is the Morialta Falls Reserve, a place much loved by Adelaide residents who, on a sunny week-end, flock there in droves. Facilities are good and there are many delightful, well-made walking tracks that meander through the reserve. As the suburbs gradually spread into the Adelaide Hills, it is becoming increasingly important to preserve some of the area's natural bushland.

FLINDERS RANGES, SOUTH AUSTRALIA

The picturesque Mount Lofty Ranges eventually give way to the dry and rugged Flinders Ranges of the north. Buckaringa Gorge, shown here, lies about 27 kilometres north of the town of Quorn. The gorge is seen at its loveliest in the summer dawn, when the slopes of craggy rock and dried grass blaze briefly in the rich gold light before slowly turning yellow-brown in the sun's strengthening rays. During the hot rainless months of summer, bushfires pose a serious threat. One spark can reduce a scene like this to a blackened wasteland.

Lakes and Rivers

The great watershed for nearly half the Australian continent is the forested Great Dividing Range, lying in the east. Its slopes give birth to a multitude of streams and rivers that carry their life-giving waters far out to the arid plains in the west. On the eastern side, after nourishing the fertile land between the ranges and the relatively small area to the coast, they empty into the Pacific Ocean. The northern end of the Great Dividing Range is in the tropics, so watercourses such as the Annan, Daintree, and Barron rivers are fed by heavy tropical rains that drench the slopes and peaks. The southern end lies in a cool temperate zone, where in winter the high ranges are crowned with snows that abundantly feed great rivers like the Snowy and the Murray. A number of the rivers are dammed, and the resulting manmade lakes are very beautiful.

Rivalling the dams in beauty are the natural lakes. Some of these, such as Queensland's Lake Eacham and Lake Barrine, are volcanic in origin; but in Tasmania many of them are glacial. Lake St Clair and Dove Lake are perhaps the best known.

At the top of the Northern Territory the east Alligator, the Katherine, and numerous other rivers rise in the Arnhem Land escarpment, an elevation of very rough and broken terrain. In the Kimberleys, to the north-west, there are even barer and more rugged ranges where some of the country's most spectacular rivers rise. One of these is the Ord River, whose colossal floodwaters are trapped by the Ord Dam in Lake Argyle. The rivers at the top end of the continent are fed by monsoonal rains that fall only between December and April. After the rain they become mighty fast-flowing watercourses that often flood widely over the plains to fill lagoons and billabongs before reaching the sea. As the moistureless Dry season sets in, the rivers gradually diminish in strength; and by November they may be again nothing more than a string of pools waiting to be replenished.

Western Australia has no range to equal the eastern watershed, and as a result this State has a much lower rainfall. The Greenough and Murchison rivers north of Perth survive on barely adequate winter rains, and rivers further north, such as the Fortescue and De Grey, may not flow properly for years. In the south-west a number of relatively small ranges give rise to several streams, the most important being the Swan-Avon River which rises on the Darling Plateau.

The rivers and lakes of the vast inland area are different again. Most of the lakes marked on the map are mere dry salt pans; and the rivers, lined with statuesque gum trees, are rivers of sand, flowing only after the occasional good rain. Rising in the few areas where ranges receive a low, erratic rainfall, the watercourses flow towards the deserts and salt lakes, but usually the insatiable sands soak up the liquid long before it reaches its destination. However, during the rare occasions when the lakes do receive an unexpected bounty, they may brim for months. Lake Eyre, which makes headlines when it fills, receives waters from a vast drainage system of some 1 240 000 square kilometres, deriving from even as far away as Cooper Creek and the Diamantina River. But most of the time Lake Eyre is thickly encrusted with glittering salt—a remarkable contrast to the sapphire softness of the mountain lakes of the east.

WALLIS LAKE, NEW SOUTH WALES

MURRAY RIVER, SOUTH AUSTRALIA

The Murray, Australia's greatest river, is of major importance to the country as a whole. Fed by a vast network of tributaries covering more than one-fifth of the continent, it is the life-blood of thousands of fertile farms now comfortably established in an area that, before irrigation, was largely sunbleached and arid. From its source in the Snowy Mountains of New South Wales, the Murray travels 2570 kilometres before entering the Southern Ocean near Goolwa in South Australia. For much of the journey through South Australia the river is bordered by colourful cliffs like these at Springcart Gully, between Renmark and Berri.

A SALT LAKE, SOUTH AUSTRALIA

This lake near Lake Albert in the south-east has dried out under the hot summer sun, leaving a crust of salt.

Following pages:
LENNARD RIVER, WESTERN AUSTRALIA

Near Fitzroy Crossing in the Kimberleys, Windjana Gorge towers over the long pools of the Lennard River, left from the time of the annual flood. At dawn the gorge is partially flooded with the sun's rays to create an eerie effect of light and shadow.

ANNAN RIVER, QUEENSLAND

Travellers cross this river twice on their way to Cooktown, on the eastern coast of Cape York Peninsula. At the first crossing, shown here, the stream is young and hurries along a rocky course marked with small waterfalls and shallow pools, some of which are ideal for swimming. The second crossing is close to Cooktown where the river, now mature, flows sluggishly under an old wooden bridge that spans its great width. Bordered with tangled, muddy mangroves, this part of the Annan presents a totally different picture from that of the earlier crossing. The river's source is in the high jungle-clad ranges just north of Bloomfield.

LAKE ARGYLE, WESTERN AUSTRALIA

This lake contains the dammed floodwaters of the Ord River, which becomes a swollen, raging watercourse after the cyclonic rains of the Wet season. The Ord Dam and the Lake Argyle tourist village, surrounded by the multi-coloured ranges of the Kimberley country, lie 67 kilometres from Kununurra. At the dam there are many vantage points from which to admire the beauty of Lake Argyle, but it is from the top lookout that the finest views are seen. Cruises run regularly on the lake, and most visitors find the cool blue expanses of water very restful after travelling through this region in the warm, dry winter months.

BLUE LAKE, SOUTH AUSTRALIA

Mount Gambier has four lovely crater lakes, but the Blue Lake is the only one that dramatically transforms its colour overnight from a dreary winter grey to brilliant blue. This phenomenon occurs every November, but in the ensuing months, between March and June, the waters gradually change back to grey again. With a depth of over 60 metres, the Blue Lake maintains the level of the sub-artesian basin and appears to be quite unaffected by the continuous pumping of water for Mount Gambier's water supply. The town itself sprawls beside the extinct volcano that contains the lakes. It provides an important centre for some of the richest farming country in the State.

DERWENT RIVER, TASMANIA

Autumn is quite the most spectacular time of the year in the New Norfolk area of the fertile Derwent Valley, for it is then that the foliage of the graceful poplar and willow trees lining the banks of the river turns to gold. The Derwent rises in Lake St Clair, a glacial lake lying in the wild mountainous country of the south-east, and enters the sea at Storm Bay. Nineteen kilometres from its mouth lies the city of Hobart, where the river is wide and deep enough to provide a superb harbour for major shipping.

NAMBUCCA RIVER, NEW SOUTH WALES

The tourist and fishing resort of Nambucca Heads is situated about 527 kilometres north of Sydney, at the entrance to this lovely river. On fine days the placid waters of the Nambucca are mirrorlike, providing clear reflections of the myriad trees lining its banks. From the elevation on which the town is built the river can be seen spreading into quiet backwaters and lagoons, just before it enters the sea. Its two branches, the Bowra River and Taylors Arm, join near Macksville to form the main stream, which then flows for only about 15 kilometres before it reaches the coast.

LAKE EILDON, VICTORIA

This lovely reservoir 137 kilometres north-east of Melbourne is filled by the Goulburn and Delatite rivers, and not only irrigates a vast area of northern Victoria, but also provides the State with hydro-electricity. At the same time it is a popular playground for aquatic enthusiasts, holidaymakers, and fishermen who are after the plentiful supplies of trout and perch. But large numbers of people come just to enjoy the superb mountain scenery that surrounds the lake. Whether the sun shines, or the misty clouds hang lazily around the wooded slopes, it is always well worth the visit.

Above:

WENLOCK RIVER, QUEENSLAND

The Wenlock River Crossing is part of the track that leads to Iron Range and the Lockhart River Mission, about 320 kilometres south of Cape York. Five minutes' walk from here lie the relics of the old gold-mining settlement of Wenlock, abandoned during the second World War. Further north, the river crosses the main route to Cape York—a ford which, for a few months after the Wet season, is very hazardous for motorists. With its banks lined with lovely riverine forest, the Wenlock, like many other rivers on Cape York Peninsula, rises in the eastern ranges and flows to the western seaboard.

Top right:

LAKE PEDDER, TASMANIA

Although the new manmade Lake Pedder is very beautiful, it was gained only with the loss of an irreplaceable natural feature of great significance. The original lake, famed for its unique beach and accessible only by a walking track, was flooded to provide this storage dam.

Bottom right:

DALY RIVER, NORTHERN TERRITORY

Upstream from the crossing is this popular camping spot, 223 kilometres south-west of Darwin.

EAST ALLIGATOR RIVER, NORTHERN TERRITORY

Cahills Crossing, about 290 kilometres east of Darwin, is in the Arnhem Land Reserve; but despite this, travellers may camp here on the western bank, provided they do not cross the river. As this spot is near the coast, the river is tidal and offers good fishing, especially at the turn of the tide. The changing tide also provides an entertaining spectacle for the onlooker, who can watch the battle for supremacy when the incoming sea-water and the downstream flow of the river meet head-on. After the sea has won, the river flows *upstream* for a while before the change takes place again.

FOGG DAM, NORTHERN TERRITORY

This earth dam 74 kilometres east of Darwin was built by the CSIRO as part of the ill-fated Humpty Doo rice-growing project that started in the 1950s. It is now an important sanctuary for a wide variety of birds, notably the honking hordes of magpie geese. Of all the accessible lagoons at the top of the Territory this is one of the best for observing birds in large numbers. Sunsets over the dam are almost invariably superb, with the glowing sun seeming to float down to the horizon in a film of cloud and haze.

The Outback

Australia's outback consists of the vast tract of sunburnt land that lies well beyond the coastal cities and the green slopes of the Great Dividing Range. Although it covers more than three-quarters of the entire continent, much of this sparsely populated region is harsh and inhospitable desert. But despite the severity of the land, there is no doubt that the 1 500 000 square kilometres of outback contain some of the most unusual and spectacular scenery in Australia.

Rising abruptly from the plains in the centre of the continent are the MacDonnell Ranges, a series of old, worn-looking elevations containing numerous gaps, chasms, and gorges of astonishing colour and beauty. The dramatic effect is increased, in some cases, by the presence of pools of still water that mirror deeply the richness of the craggy walls around them.

Much of the Centre's fascination lies in the unique monoliths rising proudly from its plains. Best known of these are the Olgas, Chambers Pillar, Mount Connor, and Ayers Rock, monarch of them all. So strange in form and beauty are these geological phenomena, that they inspire in the visitor, no matter how often he sees them, a mingled sensation of awe and astonishment. Other well-known tors, of a vastly reduced scale, are the Devils Marbles—piles of extraordinarily rounded granite boulders scattered over the land for a considerable distance.

Generally, the most accessible beauty spots at the top of the Northern Territory lie around the rivers and lagoons. During the warm, dry winter months, these delightful wooded oases offer not only respite for weary travellers but a wealth of birdlife as well.

To the west are the remote and rugged Kimberleys, a treasure-house of wild and beautiful scenery, where the colours of the landscape are even richer and more varied than in the Centre. This is the home of the grotesque bottle-shaped baobab trees, a prominent feature of the sandy plains and stony rises for about 160 kilometres inland.

Well south of the Kimberleys, but still in the far north of Western Australia, lies the Hamersley Range. Its spacious plateau is fissured by deep and precipitous gorges, their terraced walls splashed with vivid colours of chocolate, rust, and red.

Except for the south-west, most of Western Australia can be described as outback: two vast arid regions, the Great Victoria Desert and the Great Sandy Desert, claim much of the State. Much of South Australia is outback, too. Although the grim Simpson Desert, with its eternal sea of red sand-dunes, is mostly in the Northern Territory, a portion dips into South Australia. It then gives way to Sturt's Stony Desert, where vast plains of gibber stones stretch to the distant horizon. Although this desert country may appear grim and pitiless, there is superb beauty in the smooth symmetry of sculpted sand, and in the changing colours miraculously wrought by the play of light over the landscape. In good years, when the rains come, these seemingly barren regions burst into life with spectacular new plant growth.

South Australia's greatest outback scenic beauty lies in the Flinders Ranges, 300 kilometres north of Adelaide. Much of the scenery of the Flinders, with its rugged, warmly coloured ranges and superb river red gums, epitomises for many people the very essence of inland Australia.

Wide open spaces are a feature of outback New South Wales and Queensland. Here, as in the Northern Territory, peaceful billabongs and river courses are a welcome sight for eyes tired of the endless, monotonous flat plains.

BAOBAB TREES NEAR FITZROY CROSSING, WESTERN AUSTRALIA

JOFFRE GORGE, WESTERN AUSTRALIA
This gorge in the Pilbara, about 1450 kilometres north of Perth, is in the Hamersley Range, an area renowned for its rich deposits of iron ore. The range rises dramatically from the spinifex-studded plains and is topped by a wide plateau fissured with gorges whose rugged walls reveal colours of rich chocolate, rusty brown, and red. Viewed from the top, these gigantic gashes—which in some instances plummet up to 150 metres to the ground—present a more awesome sight than if seen from ground level.

NEAR GEORGETOWN, QUEENSLAND
Cattle rest by a tranquil watercourse in north-west Queensland.

Following pages:
KINGS CANYON, NORTHERN TERRITORY
Lying 370 kilometres south-west of Alice Springs, this magnificent gorge is the largest and most spectacular in Central Australia. Its colossal walls tower over the valley floor to 182 metres, dwarfing giant boulders, trees, and man alike.

STANDLEY CHASM, NORTHERN TERRITORY

This grand chasm in the MacDonnell Ranges, just over 50 kilometres west of Alice Springs, is one of the most popular with sightseers in Central Australia. Access is easy: from the car park a delightful and relatively short walking path winds through the rocky hills. The chasm is perhaps best seen at midday, when the walls are suffused with rich colours of gold and red; but it is splendid at almost any time of the day, its rocky surfaces glowing with warm reflected light. This vast cleavage averages a width of about four metres and towers to a height of well over 60 metres.

ROE CREEK, NORTHERN TERRITORY

In the Dry season, Roe Creek is nothing more than a series of shallow pools that will gradually dry out under the hot sun unless replenished by further rains. The creek, which passes through Honeymoon Gap in the western MacDonnells, near Alice Springs, is typical of many outback watercourses. In times of flood its character is changed completely: the peace is shattered by the sound of rushing water tumbling past the river red gums, taking with it fallen trees, debris, and anything in its path. In the gap near by, there are some very interesting varieties of rock strata.

Above:

PARACHILNA GORGE, SOUTH AUSTRALIA

Parachilna, one of many beautiful gorges in the Flinders Ranges, lies near the small settlement of Blinman. In springtime, flowering wattles grace the banks of the creek and dot the slopes of the surrounding hills. The creek usually has a small amount of water in it, unless there has been an unusually long dry spell. Although the Flinders begin in the rolling hills near Crystal Brook, most people think of Quorn, 325 kilometres north of Adelaide, as the gateway to the ranges. Some of the loveliest scenery starts here, continuing up to Wilpena, Aroona Valley, and Parachilna Gorge.

Top right:

AYERS ROCK, NORTHERN TERRITORY

One of the great wonders of the world, this awesome rock has a circumference of nine-and-a-half kilometres, and towers 317 metres over the surrounding plain.

Bottom right:

THE OLGAS, NORTHERN TERRITORY

Lying 32 kilometres west of Ayers Rock, the Olgas are an extraordinary and unique group of sandstone monoliths that over the ages have been fashioned by the elements into domes. This impressive view is from the Katajuta Lookout.

MATARANKA, NORTHERN TERRITORY

Set in a small reserve on Mataranka Station and surrounded by lovely palms and stately pandanus, this thermal pool is like a small oasis in the hot and usually arid far north. The water temperature of 33°C may seem rather warm for swimming when the day temperature is about the same, but it is surprisingly refreshing. Upstream is the head of a spring where crystal-clear water wells up from a deep underground basin to fill both this pool and a much smaller pond full of exquisite plantlife. Mataranka is situated about five kilometres off the Stuart Highway, south of Katherine.

GLEN HELEN GORGE, NORTHERN TERRITORY

To appreciate the full extent of Glen Helen's beauty, one must be up at dawn, walking along the banks of the long waterhole just as the sun's first rays glimmer on the face of the cliff. In the stillness of the morning, the wonderfully vibrant colours of the gorge are mirrored in the pool to create a scene of memorable grandeur. This is one place in Central Australia where visitors are bound to hear the mournful nightly songs of the dingoes—and campers may well have one howling outside their tents! Glen Helen Gorge lies 127 kilometres west of Alice Springs.

DESERT WILDFLOWERS, SOUTH AUSTRALIA

After good rains the deserts of Australia burst into miraculous new growth, displaying carpets of brightly-coloured wildflowers that extend to the far horizon. This display of poached-egg daisies and billy buttons is at the Kopperamanna Crossing of Cooper Creek where it crosses the Birdsville Track, one of the most infamous routes of the outback. Characterised by rolling sand-dunes, seas of gibbers, cheerless claypans, and a few isolated homesteads, the road runs for 489 kilometres, from Marree in South Australia to Birdsville in Queensland. For this entire distance there are no supplies of petrol or stores.

CORDILLO DOWNS, SOUTH AUSTRALIA

On Cordillo Downs Station, situated in the far north-eastern corner of South Australia by one of the loneliest roads in the country, there are many spectacular sand-dunes. Varying in colour from pale pink to rich red, the dunes stretch far into Sturt's Stony Desert, breaking the monotony of flat sand and cruel gibber plains with stones varying in size from small pebbles to large jagged rocks. At sunrise and sunset these dunes are magically transformed into ruby hills of glowing splendour.

EDITH FALLS, NORTHERN TERRITORY

These falls, part of the Edith River, lie 27 kilometres off the Stuart Highway, at the end of a fairly rough track north of Katherine. They are now incorporated in a national park. A walking track leads to the spot where a series of waterfalls cascades over rocky walls into deep pools of clear water surrounded with tropical vegetation. Near the main pool, shown here, a camping ground is situated. Like all the watercourses of the north, the Edith River and the falls become raging torrents during the Wet season when the floodwaters come down.

KATHERINE CAVE, NORTHERN TERRITORY

Managed by the Northern Territory Reserves Board, this limestone cave with its fantastic formations is part of the Katherine Sixteen Mile Cave Reserve, near Katherine. The reserve boasts a fascinating guided tour that leads visitors through natural bushland. In the Dry season, when the caves are comfortably cool and dry, cave tours are led by the ranger, an experienced speleologist. During the Wet, the ground absorbs the heavy rains so that water percolates down through the cavern roofs in an unceasing staccato of drops. The air in the caves at this time is thick with humidity, and periodically the chambers are flooded, so that viewing is impossible.

Wilderness

For its size, Australia is very sparsely populated; and although a large portion of the land is used for primary industry, many wilderness areas still exist. All these areas differ enormously from one another, but every one, in its own way, is infinitely precious to us today.

Some of the most spectacular untamed country lies deep in the mountains of Tasmania, Victoria, and New South Wales. Well away from the regular tourist routes of the arid MacDonnell Ranges in Central Australia, there are many awe-inspiring gorges and high ridges providing marvellous views for the more adventurous. The Flinders Ranges, too, have areas of little-known beauty, particularly in the far north at Arkaroola and in the Gammon Ranges.

Different again is the wilderness of the desert regions—the Simpson Desert, with its barrier of red sand-dunes swelling from the plains like ocean waves, or Sturt's Stony Desert with its stark gibber plains changing in colour from warm reds to hard steel greys according to the angle of light. But the strangest area of all is the Pinnacles Desert in Western Australia, where thousands of limestone pinnacles loom over many hectares of golden sands. The sand is held together by a delicate crust of what look like petrified roots, some scattered over the ground, others erect like small sandy stalagmites. Once crushed underfoot, they are lost forever, and so it is fortunate for the preservation of the desert that access is not easy. The track leading in to this extraordinary wilderness area is full of rocks so large that even driving a vehicle with exceptionally good clearance is like navigating a boat through a treacherous coral reef.

Many Australians now realise the importance of wilderness. The conservation of the ecology in such regions means much more than just protecting the flora and fauna for future generations to enjoy—although this in itself is very important. But areas untouched by man serve as essential laboratories for research work in medicine, agriculture, and commerce. Natural vegetation plays a very important part both in protecting the land from erosion, and, in catchment areas, aiding and facilitating water storage. Further, as more and more people are beginning to discover, the beauty of wilderness offers an excellent panacea for the tensions and troubles of our highly complex modern society.

Yet the areas of wilderness are shrinking. Each year many hectares of natural bushland are destroyed either by developers or by the over-grazing of stock. Consequently the preservation of land and adequate control by patrolling rangers is vitally important. Although there are at present quite a number of national parks and reserves throughout Australia, many of them protect only a tiny portion of land. More areas are constantly proposed for conservation—some of these, such as the rainforests of tropical Queensland, being already in urgent need of protection. Access to some national parks is very difficult, but others have bitumen roads leading to their periphery, where tourist facilities have been established. From there networks of walking paths lead into the park. In the wilder parts of desert and coastline, and in the Kimberleys and Arnhem Land, the best protection lies in remoteness. In many such areas—for the time being, at least—access by vehicle is either extremely difficult or well nigh impossible.

STURT'S STONY DESERT AFTER RAIN, SOUTH AUSTRALIA

MORAN FALLS, QUEENSLAND

The Moran Falls are situated on the Lamington Plateau which rises high above the Queensland-New South Wales border in the McPherson Range, south of Brisbane. This spectacular veil of water cascades down 80 metres of sheer rock, over moisture-loving mosses and ferns whose brilliant green colours are partially screened in a film of mist. Access is by a walking path winding through sub-tropical rainforest for about one-and-a-half kilometres from the main road to O'Reillys. The superb vegetation of this area is just as much an attraction for visitors as are the falls themselves.

MOUNT HOWITT, VICTORIA

Snow gums are found on all the higher slopes of the mountains in the Alps. This fine one stands beside the hiking trail on Mount Howitt. Rising to 1742 metres, Mount Howitt lies north of Licola and is linked by a trail to Mount Buller, some 16 kilometres away.

Following pages:
PINNACLES DESERT, WESTERN AUSTRALIA

Erosion has exposed these weird limestone spires which are part of the Nambung National Park, north of Perth.

ARKAROOLA, SOUTH AUSTRALIA

The view from Sillers Lookout, on the Ridgetops Road, is typical of the far north of the Flinders Ranges. The road leading to the lookout was constructed by a mining company while searching for uranium. A navigational challenge, it winds tortuously along the tops of the mountain ridges, some of them edged like razors with sheer slopes plummetting to the valleys below. Today the management at the Arkaroola Village has taken over the maintenance of the road which, for safety reasons, is closed to the public. The incredibly steep grades can be safely negotiated only by special four-wheel-drive vehicles, which are available on tour from the village.

MONSOONAL RAINFOREST, QUEENSLAND

Lying between Bamaga and Somerset, at the top of Cape York Peninsula, there are some lovely patches of monsoonal rainforest. Unlike tropical rainforest, which requires large quantities of rain over most of the year, monsoonal vegetation is nourished only by the substantial rains that fall between November and April. For the rest of the year it is kept damp by the prevailing moisture-laden clouds. Contrary to popular belief, rainforest covers less than one per cent of Cape York Peninsula. Apart from the narrow strip that runs from Cardwell to Cooktown, there are only isolated patches in the north.

CARNARVON GORGE, QUEENSLAND

The Carnarvon Gorge is part of the Consuelo Tableland which rises to over 915 metres and forms part of the Great Dividing Range. Situated 745 kilometres north-west of Brisbane, this comparatively undeveloped national park is a paradise for the explorer, botanist, geologist, zoologist, and anthropologist. Throughout the gorge towering sandstone cliffs with rugged basalt crowns rise up over the limpid waters of Carnarvon Creek. There is a wonderful variety of vegetation: of particular interest are some very ancient Macrozamia palms, whose growth rate is only 30 centimetres in 100 years. All sightseeing must be done on foot, along walking tracks in the gorge itself. The main path, based on old cattle pads, follows the creek and crosses it many times. It is a well-marked trail, with signs indicating creek crossings and side tracks that lead to such interesting places as the Moss Gardens, Violet Gorge, the Hell Hole, the Cathedral, and the Art Gallery, which contains some fine examples of Aboriginal art.

GOSSES BLUFF, NORTHERN TERRITORY

Lying in a remote area at the western end of the MacDonnell Ranges, about 60 kilometres west of Hermannsburg, Gosses Bluff resembles a gigantic pound or amphitheatre. Its spacious valley, which in spring is covered in a profusion of flowering plants, is surrounded by a ring of bare, craggy ranges that tower up to 300 metres over the vast plains, falling away only in one small place to allow entry. The track into the valley is very rough and is broken in places by washaways. The question of how the bluff was formed has aroused much speculation, but unfortunately a great deal of the evidence of its origin has disappeared over the ages. Some say that it is a geological fluke, but a more popular theory is that the crater-like formation is a gigantic scar caused by an asteroid hurtling in from outer space. From the air it certainly looks like a star wound; and if it is, Gosses Bluff must be one of the largest craters thus formed on the earth's surface. Whatever its origins, it is a very beautiful and interesting place.

MARRAKAI, NORTHERN TERRITORY

This channel lined with bamboo and freshwater mangroves is one of many that drain the Marrakai Plain and flow into the Adelaide River, south-east of Darwin. Just a little upstream from here the creek suddenly opens out to the vast plain. Here herds of buffaloes roam beside enormous flocks of wild birds —brolgas, ibises, jabirus, and egrets —that rise when disturbed in a splendid flurry of feathers. In the creeks and in the Adelaide River there are plenty of saltwater crocodiles, which can often be seen basking on the muddy banks. Access to this area is only by boat.

WILSONS PROMONTORY, VICTORIA

Dwarfing both man and vegetation, these monstrous tors, known as the Mussolini Rocks, stand majestically on the hillside overlooking the walking track to Waterloo Bay. Rocks are very much a feature of the area, which is one of the most popular national parks in Australia for hikers and nature lovers. Each year thousands walk the many paths that wind through the hills and gullies and along the beautiful shores. Situated in Gippsland, 240 kilometres south-east of Melbourne, the promontory juts into the waters of Bass Strait to form the most southerly point of the Australian mainland.

CRADLE MOUNTAIN, TASMANIA

The jagged peaks of Cradle Mountain, which rears up at the end of the glacial Dove Lake in the central highlands, reach to around 1500 metres. The mountain is part of a national park that extends as far as Lake St Clair in the south, the two lakes being linked by a hiking track. The park also has many other walking paths that lead to places of tremendous beauty. One of the greatest hazards for hikers here is the weather, because even in summer, snow and severe storms can suddenly sweep over the land. It is essential for all-day walkers to register their route with the ranger.